The Owl and the Pussycat

The Owl
and the
Pussycat

by Edward Lear

Illustrated by Jan Brett

SIMON & SCHUSTER

LONDON • SYDNEY • NEW YORK • TOKYO • SINGAPORE • TORONTO

First published in Great Britain in 1991 by
Simon & Schuster Young Books
Simon & Schuster Limited
Wolsey House
Wolsey Road
Hemel Hempstead
Herts. HP2 4SS

First published in the USA in 1991 by G.P. Putnam's Sons,
This edition published by arrangement with G.P. Putnam's Sons.
a division of The Putnam & Grosset Book Group, New York, USA.

Set in 24pt. Bembo educational by Goodfellow & Egan, Cambridge
Printed and bound in Belgium by Proost International Book Production

British Library Cataloguing in Publication Data
Lear, Edward 1812–1888
    The Owl and the Pussycat
    I. Title   II. Brett, Jan
    821.8

ISBN 0-7500-0773-7
ISBN 0-7500-0774-5 pbk

For Lia

The Owl and the Pussycat went to sea
In a beautiful pea-green boat:

They took some honey, and plenty
of money
Wrapped up in a five-pound note.

The Owl looked up to the stars above,
And sang to a small guitar,

"O lovely Pussy, O Pussy, my love,
What a beautiful Pussy you are,
    You are,
    You are!
What a beautiful Pussy you are!"

Pussy said to the owl, "You elegant fowl,
How charmingly sweet you sing!

Oh! let us be married; too long we have tarried:
ut what shall we do for a ring?"

They sailed away, for a year and a day,

To the land where the bong-tree grows;

And there in a wood a Piggy-wig stood,
With a ring at the end of his nose,
    His nose,
    His nose,
With a ring at the end of his nose.

"Dear Pig, are you willing to sell for
one shilling
Your ring?" Said the Piggy, "I will."

So they took it away, and were married next d
By the Turkey who lives on the hill.

They dined on mince and slices of quince,
Which they ate with a runcible spoon;

And hand in hand, on the edge of the sand,
They danced by the light of the moon,
The moon,
The moon,
They danced by the light of the moon.